METAL

BookLife

written by
Harriet Brundle

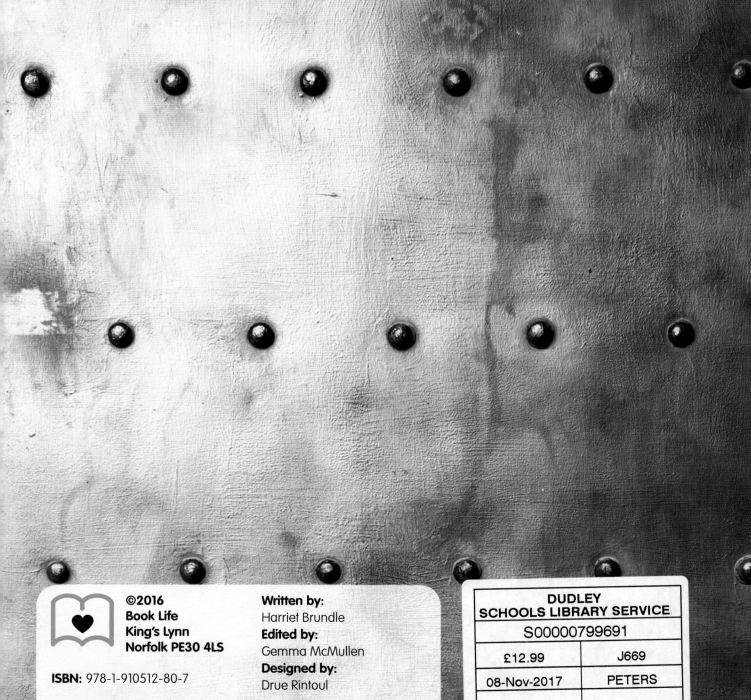

©2016
Book Life
King's Lynn
Norfolk PE30 4LS

ISBN: 978-1-910512-80-7

Written by:
Harriet Brundle
Edited by:
Gemma McMullen
Designed by:
Drue Rintoul

A catalogue record for this book
is available from the British Library.

Contents

The blue words in this book can be found in the glossary on page 23.

What is a Material?

Materials are what things are made of.
Some materials are natural and some are man-made.

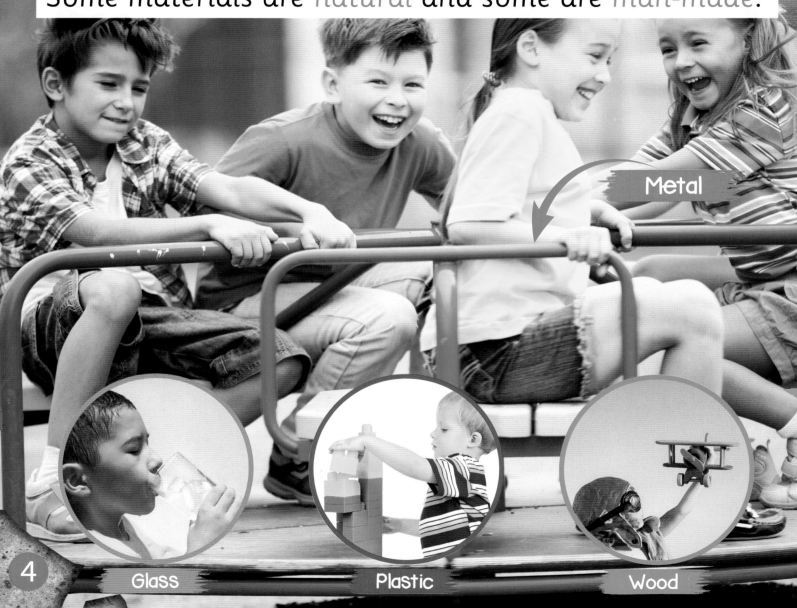

Metal

Glass

Plastic

Wood

Every material has its own properties. A material might be very soft. This would be one of its properties.

Pyjamas, cuddly toys and pillows are all soft.

What is Metal?

Metal is a natural material. It is found inside rocks. When the rocks are heated, the metal can be separated.

TRY THIS!
· · · · · · · · · · ·
Have a look around the classroom. What can you see that might be made of metal?

There are lots of different types of metal. Each of the different types of metal has its own name.

Copper

These are just a few types of metal.

Bronze

Silver

Aluminium

Platinum

Gold

Properties of Metal

Some metals are very hard and strong. Steel and iron are so strong they are used to make buildings and bridges!

Steel

Some types of metal are very soft and bendy. Aluminium is used to make drinks cans which can be easily squashed.

What is Metal Used For?

Metal has hundreds of different uses. Cars, bikes and even aeroplanes are made from metal.

Aeroplane

Can you think of anything else that is made from metal?

Gold and silver are called precious types of metal.
They are harder to find and cost a lot of money to buy.

Gold and silver are used to make jewellery.

Metal in Water

When metal gets wet, it goes rusty. When a metal has gone rusty, it looks orange and feels rough.

A rusty car

Metal can be painted or sprayed to protect it from water. This stops it getting rusty.

Metal in Heat

When some metals are heated, they become soft enough to be bent.

Be careful not to burn your legs on a hot slide!

When the metal is hot enough, it is bent to make different things. A horseshoe is made by bending metal.

Magnetic Metal

Some types of metal are magnetic. When a magnet is put near a magnetic metal, it draws the metal to it.

Iron is a type of metal that is magnetic. Paper clips and scissors are made of iron.

Musical Instruments

Some musical instruments are made from metal. The metal is often polished to make it very shiny.

Trumpets and saxophones are both made of a metal called brass. They are called brass instruments.

Trumpet

Saxophone

Can you think of any other instruments that belong to the brass family?

Recycling Metal

Some types of metal can be recycled, which means we can use them again. We should try to recycle to help the environment.

This symbol means that a material can be recycled.

Aluminium can be recycled. Empty cans should be taken to special recycling banks so they can be melted down and used again.

Fun Facts

DID YOU KNOW?

There are 91 different types of metal!

Experiment

Find 6 things that are made from metal in your classroom. Look at their properties. Are they stiff or bendy? Are they shiny or dull?

The centre of Planet Earth is made from iron, which is a metal!

Glossary

Magnetic
Something that is pulled towards a magnet.

Man-made
Something that is made by humans.

Natural
Something that has been made by nature.

Properties
The different qualities of a material.

Rust
A crumbly orange material made when metal gets wet.

Index

Photocredits: Abbreviations: l-left, r-right, b-bottom, t-top, c-centre, m-middle. All images are courtesy of Shutterstock.com.
Front Cover m - sigurcamp. Front cover bl, 21tm - thelefty. Front cover bm, 19r - DenisFilm. Front cover br, 8 - ventdusud. 2 - kkymek. 3 - Roman Sigaev. 4 - Pressmaster. 4bl - 3445128471. 4bm - Temych. 4br - Sunny studio. 5l - wavebreakmedia. 5r - hartphotography. 6inset - Fokin Oleg. 6br - huyangshu. 7br - Dim Dimich. 7tr - Jesus Keller. 7m - Fablok. 7tl - Yegor Larin. 7bl - ppart. 7m - Ilizia. 9, 21br - tobkatrina. 10 - muratart. 11 - Carolyn Franks. 11inset - Mikhail Tchkheidze. 12 - Fotokor77. 12inset - Lasse Ansaharju. 13 - sydeen. 14 - Lasse Ansaharju. 15r - Fotokostic. 15inset - Catherine311. 16inset - MilanB. 16br - Morrowind. 17 - Alan Bailey. 18bl - Anton Havelaar. 18tr - Berents. 19l - Jaimie Duplass. 19r - DenisFilm. 20 - OgnjenO. 20inset - Roman Sigaev. 21bl - Switlana Yaremenko. 22tl - Your Design. 22bl - Lukiyanova Natalia / frenta. 22r - donatas1205.